THE AGE OF BRIGGS & STRATTON

THE AGE OF
BRIGGS & STRATTON

(HAMMERTOWN BOOK 2)

PETER CULLEY

VANCOUVER

NEW STAR BOOKS

2008

NEW STAR BOOKS LTD.
107 − 3477 Commercial Street
Vancouver, BC V5N 4E8   CANADA

1517 − 1574 Gulf Road
Point Roberts, WA 98281   USA

www.NewStarBooks.com
info@NewStarBooks.com

"Publication of this work is made possible by grants from the Canada
Council, the Department of Canadian Heritage, the Province of British
Columbia, and the British Columbia Arts Council.

Parts of this book have appeared as an issue of *Tolling Elves* and in *The
Capilano Review*.

Designed by Mark Timmings
Designed by Timmings & Debay Design
Cover concept & artwork by Roy Arden
Printed on 100% post-consumer recyled paper
Printed and bound in Canada by Gauvin Press
First printing, April 2008

LIBRARY AND ARCHIVES CANADA CATALOGUING IN PUBLICATION

Culley, Peter, 1958 −
    The age of Briggs & Stratton / Peter Culley.

Poems.
ISBN 978-1-55420-039-9

    1. Nanaimo (B.C.) — Poetry. I. Title.
PS8555.U48A74 2008   C811'.54   C2008−900077−3

for Daphne

DOWSING FOR DUMMIES

In memoriam
Robert Creeley

'... a tall, lank, uncouth looking person,
long hair hanging over his face,
a queue down his back tied with an eel skin ...'
       (Albert Gallatin on Andrew Jackson)

I. MARSHALL, NC

Just enough iron
in my forehead

to divert
from the middle distance

the moth
in its path,

not enough
to avoid
by moonlight

the back porch's
sudden double step

a beavertail slap
resounding, lodged

in the elbow
an unreachable itch
rather than pain
per se —

(the intimate
two-handed
grip of the stranger
steadying herself
on me
the aisle man)

at the depot
the Sheriff
dispenses silence

with onions, a mustard-
coloured raffle ticket

folded to a point
of de facto forfeiture

as outside the window
the French Broad River

recedes in mercury loops
unnavigably,
in either direction.

II.

In the two minutes
of pale green dime-sized

light left to us
by the lightning bugs'

impact against the windshield,
let us open the first volume

of our Blue Pelican
Animals Without Backbones

to the illustration
of animal light

which is a one and a half inch
square sepiatone gravure

with the words
animal light lit

by a glow-worm's
animal light.

III. ALL THE DOPES HE COULD DRINK
(Sodom Laurel Album)

sip apple juice and icemelt
and icemelt and ice-
melt and icemelt and icemelt

sweet sweet sweet sweet tea
sweet sweet sweet sweet sweet sweet tea
sweet sweet sweet sweet tea

peach Nehi over the Laurel falls, Cheerwine,
the unnamed second best orange pop
ever after Narvik Fanta

a tangerine kick
through undiagnosed veins
with black floaters

spelling your name
'*Bonjour Tristesse*'
when Jean Seberg's narration

moved from compromised
monochrome
present to a blue 'scope past

impressive even
on pan'n'scan VHS
for its unblinking

existentialist noonday,
no thirst therefore
no beverages till cocktails

at the casino, no picnics
not even the Sirkean
consolation of objects

just the stairs to the beach
a foreground agreement,
a narrow recession,

an unplugged record player
that had earlier spun
Georges Auric's 1958 pre-Shankar

version of teenage ambient
the kind someone might remember
in a narration

who'd suppressed
(as I this Yoo-hoo coloured river)
everything else.

IV. RECORDS ARE LIKE LIFE

The ageing shuffle function's
approximation of taste
gave us six downers in a row

then bounced back
with the cracker-barrel rictus
of happy hardcore.

Sadly never so 'wasted'
that it ever made sense to me
just as in 1978 you could slip 'new wave'

records on when everyone was drunk —
Homicide by 999, say, or The Stranglers (*Peaches*),
but ... The shuffle function was

letting anyone else do it
which was never.
The shuffle function

of the guidance counsellor's
high-freckled 'rap'
about the 'sidjuation'

tight Jimmy Olsen curls
into an Archie crosshatch fade
a bifocal lowering sans specs

comes to rest
at the bridge of your nose, says
down to business —

and so impressive
the audio-visual gestetner
ink-smelling gestalt

(until perhaps a half-dozen
years ago I would still roam the halls
in sleep, stealing books

in an admixture of revulsion
that when I awoke) ...
that lacking even a robot's

will to charm the odds
or even an 8-track or a Lazy Susan
I consumed the script.

V. DOUBLE DEADTIME BUMMER BLUES
(Judee Sill)

Alive to the moment
but you sleep a lot,

'misspent' as in
Stevenson describing

an unexpected skill
at pool or cards —though

an incremental embrace
of criminality inevitable

given just how strict, &c.
Dimes for the parking meter

in bowls at the Bank of
Montreal downtown (now

gone, the Harewood branch
gone) those little dusty mints

as we left the taverna
just as everyone's back was turned;

coffee with Coffeemate
at the Caledonia Clinic —

brighter now, flooded everywhere
with glare it would be harder

to disappear into that soft-fringed
theology, those Townsite

alleys empty at all hours
of everything but

Il Quatro Staggioni
The Sickness Unto Death

VI. ROADRUNNER

('I'm in love with moonlight,
128 when it's dark outside')

Though my infantilised cat
confirms my existence
the cars don't see me —

Ganesha's prints
were all over the trunk, giant

pants in black
with a velcroed
right-turn indicator

over which
a cuff neatly folded,
red compact, splashed,

lost, speeding, between Boundary
& Bowen, the other leg muddy,
raggedy, platforms

worn at an angle of 35 degrees
from walking in circles —
just right for ditch baloney,

though between here and
the 'quarter mile'
of the old Northfield industrial park

(mid-sixties, still an implied
roundedness in the signage, moderne
so far as it recalls *Rockford*,

Barnaby Jones &c.) the
fairgrounds, concrete
terraces overlooking

the oval track, everywhere
the cars had been before me
writing through the ivy.

VII. ROADS TO FREEDOM

In a basement
presently bereft of life

avocado
beer fridge contains single

serving Pop Shoppe
Tom Collins mix bottle

to which the cap
bent by the opener

is reattached
precariously and

symbolically
panelling well you know

old tube TV
21 inch black and

white and best of
all an RCA in

jack to which I
could run a chord from

the portable
suitcase mono that was

my parent's thus
adding a channel of deep

mahogany
courtesy the TV's

mighty twin four
inch cones resonating

through layers of made-
in-Canada-goddam

it-Verathane
and varnished returned now

to duty as
the downstairs TV which

I alone watched
things in black and white old

movies &c.
on this warm night having

drained the mix which
when held long enough gave

a hint of fizz —
good & cold certainly!

I returned to the
weekday summer showing of

the early 70's
serialisation

of Sartre's *Roads*
to Freedom done by

the BBC
in that particular

house style that
English actors use

portraying
the French as in that great

Maigret series
with Michael Gambon

of which nothing
outside a lot of shouted

conversations
I remember nothing

except for that
on this night the action

suddenly shrank
to the size of a postcard

then a stamp
then a pearl on which you

could still make out
the tiny figure of a

woman in a
trench coat striding across

a tiny room
then the image brightened

to the head
of a pin retinal

trace only now
and then from the back of

the TV an
acrid plume of black smoke

(*commitment*
they were talking about)

poured clinging
through the vent upstairs yanked

the plug blue blue
spark a copper smell curled

but the chancy
wiring and fridge were saved.

VIII. FLOW, LAURA NIAGARA

. . . when I was a Freeport
and you were the main drag . . .

. . . I've got a lot of patience, baby
that's a lot of patience to lose . . .
   (LAURA NYRO)

. . . affectionate
machine-tickling aphid . . .
   (DARWIN)

globalisation's
over-crayoned blue sky flakes

but the duck's left blank,
like Depot Harbour, Ontario

getting rubbed off
the grid was no biblical

judgement, dig —
it looked like a nice place!

but Carthage now
looks better than this place

fifty years on —
alder-poked, broom-worried,

a ghost town
after the ghost had gone —

a desertedness
out of large-print SF —

writhing and plinking
in the furzy foundation

the dreaded
ukelelekonig

laced its tongue
through a web

of taut nylon but
we couldn't make it out

or if it was even
talking at all —

auctioned out
from under your feet

like the family
Astrakhan, and if

a trestle is the only
thing holding it back

then admit the jungle
the empire of the ants

could we not just
get it over with?

Or must we choke forever
on periphery's piney sap?

IX. BRACTON: DE LEGIBUS ET CONSUETUDINIBUS ANGLIAE (1250)

For if they settle
in my tree
they are no more mine —

before I shut them
into a hive —
than are the birds

who make their nest there,
and therefore
if another hives them

he will be their owner.
A swarm that flies
out of my hive

is taken to be mine
so long as it remains
in my sight

and pursuit is not impossible,
otherwise it becomes
the property of the taker.

Just but one bee
on the paler
other kind of

sweet-pea, orange
chevron very
circa '83, &

you'd think the boys
at Last Call Towing
would be glad to

see their girlriends
(Wednesday PM
half-cloudy

scented August)
but they won't climb
down or let go

their pneumatic
bolt-tighteners
long enough

and won't discuss
who said what to
who last weekend

on innertubes
that flattered them
but made us look

like our dads, tits
up on the couch
and these maroon

uniforms itch
more and more as
threadbare summer

wears out its buzz
and welcome mat
and baseball hat.

X. LAST OF THE MOHICANS

Good country this
for lazy fellows
(wrote Wilson from

Kentucky); *they plant*
corn, turn their
pigs into the

woods and in
the autumn feed upon
corn and pork.

They lounge about
the rest of the year.
But sometime between

then and now,
despite flip books,
Jack Spicer bootlegs,

Miltown, Motown, Milton
the race of tavern
loafers, customs-house flaneurs

wall holder-uppers
& Virginia eye-gougers
died out, wagons

full of keeners,
enthusiasts, stereoptical
estimaters & paint-chip

matchers darkened
the passes, planting apples
for roughage not cider.

XI. POPULAR CHARACTERISTICS

(1800) (Henry Adams)

That free-born
Rhode Islanders ought
never to submit

to be priest-ridden,
nor to pay for
the privilege

of travelling
on the highway.
Better indeed stranded

up to our
rusticated Yankee necks
in yellow shit

than travel
to Providence
under such pretenses;

wearing a horse collar,
a T-shirt reading
'Citizen X' —

better a propellered beanie,
a New Year's diaper,
a Brownie uniform —

and if the bones
of any shiny Hussar,
uncowed by Miranda v. Arizona

or the fourth amendment
or the by-God
Yosemite Sam mudflaps

hanging from my ears
attempt to stroll unbidden
into my library,

garage or sugar shack
they will end as struts
in the drug tunnel

that gently winds
between Lasqueti Island
and Narraganset Bay:—

XII. MAMA ROUX

At the corner store
the Protestant Santeria
of the lottery logos —

fake foxing
against a gold rush font,
the leprechaun's derby

overflows —
a yellow cord
marks off the liquor store

after eleven,
outside (courtesy of
the smoke from Burns Bog)

the moon trails
a gambler's beard,
a kettle of coins

rattles inside the aqua
tunnel under highway one,
illuminates the figure eight

I inscribed on a whim
on the slope outside
the Cranberry Firehall —

or it could be
the Pimpjuice sticker
the Pepsico rep

slapped near the entrance
or the icecube with wings
and a Grecian profile

loyal to the old regime
where the word 'cold'
came wreathed in beads of sweat

and every word
unashamedly itself,
like those farmers

in Emerson
who planted
themselves last

pulling the earth
over themselves
like an old quilt.

XIII.

Talk about me if you please
but I must be Hercules . . .
(ALLEN TOUSSAINT)

September 'tox
and the 'sub-conscious'
back with pearly teeth,
party dreams as
subtle as *Marnie*
without the saving grace
of a young Bruce Dern,
otherwise a pipeload
of nasty eighties
bowl-scrapings
filtered through a screen
of Screen, the fear
is not of crystal meth
but access
to wakefulness
via household products
otherwise divvied
up among fighter crews,
prison guards, janitors
and the federales
of Sumas
patrolling beet fields
for sugar thieves.

XIV. MOUNTAIN MUSIC

(Riley Puckett)

The fiddle, the yodel, the harmonica & the fife,
The drumskin, the flintlock, pack animal & knife,
The zither, the whistle and autoharp give life —
A great eye fluttering open in the deep forested host
Driving back Covenant, Cherokee, revenue's ghost.

The 78, the 33 & the 45 spin like
The rhododendron holler on its axis, to survive
Means breathing the dissonance like so much pollen, not to
    fit
The rosin to the bridge or the finger to the mercury mind
Is to awake in an ancestor's grip, so clammy and unkind.

The singing dead glide through the layers as if tunnelling to
    France,
Their keening like the insect wail of an old thermos; to
    dance
Like Bobby did, with one hand waving, shark-like above the
    shit-
Strewn beach of history — as they say 'free' — to
    unencumbered crawl
Beneath barbed wire, past parish dogs & round the bloody
    wall.

XV. MOUNTAIN MUSIC

Thus a jug
appeared on stage
at their various

performances
but purely
for effect.

Lean'n'Pernod
after your mother's funeral,
(Adventist?) later kitefights

at Piper's Lagoon —
luckily the barnacles
were their own antidote,

though not
to the ugly vintages of
the beerstrike summer,

picking little
Gregory Pecks
out of my belly

for months afterward,
scattered now
(those of us permitted to live!)

from the Palatinate of Prince Rupert
to the free city
of Holberg —

& as at the end of side two, today —
cresting the hill at Dogland,
Harewood below

a dusty *deshabillé* backdrop
out of Sigmund Romberg
in the last actinic orange

August sunrise
of the Trudeau administration —
none of our concern.

XVI. FRAGMENT OF LETTER, FEMALE HANDWRITING, FOUND WALKING BACK FROM THE CORNER STORE, OCT. 2, 2005

can one
like to do
how we
did not
as friends

(reverse)

my attititude
going for
be more
good as
asked me

The dewy or was it shimmer
rising off the stand of wild
mint under the Catstream bridge,

sparse sleepy Toytown traffic
waddling up up the hill
past the firestation, the diner

where you worked,
unmatched vivacity in
a city of incandescent

waitresses, these gabled houses, through
brown fences a tobacco corona
ringed round stucco under a

jutting pipe, were insufficient,
weasel words, false memories —
backed into a corner

I emptied the dandelion wine
discreetly onto the ground,
less empathetic than the rock

I'd stumbled over,
reconstructing leaks
from instant coffee in the margins,

and a theory of everything
that didn't account
for walking downhill,

the age of Laing gave way to
the age of Foucault
while we slept, the flapping

muslin curtains and fairy lights
all I remember of the heatwave,
& if on that night I'd drowned

your sleek otter dive
would have been my unearned
Polaroid epitaph.

XVII. A LETTER FROM HAMMERTOWN TO A PAIR OF UNSPECIFIED BROOKLYN POSTAL DISTRICTS

Do you have
The Magic Band

audience tape, LA Troubadour,
Boxing Day '76,

(audio quality:
better than the Dead Sea scrolls,

not quite as good
as one of those Northern Soul

anthologies taken
from singles

traded for leapers
in the ozone-swept alleys

of Cleethorpes?)
The punters energized,

better fed than usual,
at least the day before —

those from the area
and those like Mr. Van Vliet

swept in on the *franzklines*
and Santa Anas —

it takes a day for the stuffing
and unfamiliar liqueurs

to clear but everyone
hits the ground running —

a mellotron is introduced
the clarinet is busted out

& the old songs wriggle
& roll like the Ford-era traffic outside

recreating the accidents
of their conception —

The Blimp in this context
greeted like *Katmandu*

or *Kashmir*, old pros
with a hint of indifference

givin' it to the people
like the last present

hidden forgotten behind
the tree, though at points

the rust flakes off
to dust mite central

blowing back yo-yos
tumbleweeds, poppies, coyotes.

XVIII. ACADIAN DRIFTWOOD

There is no use
crying about it,
Cousin America
has run off with
a Presbyterian
parson, and that
is the end of it.
    (HORACE WALPOLE)

The beaver, the rampike, the musket, the cod,
The fortress of pine & the hovel of sod,
Orcadian whalemen possessed by a God
Merciless, English, a bit of a sod.

The nickel, the loonie, the quarter, the toonie,
McDonald, Trudeau, Pearson, Mulroney,
Only Diefenbaker made us swoon, we
Liked his rhetoric on the noon TV.

Poetry arrived in the year of '65,
A taterdemalion just barely alive,
He went out to Horseshoe Bay on a drive
And left us a goal for which we should strive.

XIX. A LETTER FROM HAMMERTOWN TO FORT TRYON

My exoskelton
protects my tongue

but leaves my
hindquarters exposed,

if only to the weather:
my country,

created by the dry stroke
of a Whitehall pen

for the benefit of haberdashers
and fishmongers

saw the draft resisters
as a rich source.

of mental pelts
for acid testing

and the carbonation
of Lake Erie,

Vancouver was the
first city

to banish Lenny Bruce
ship back the Sikhs &c.

& skim the foam
from the cappuccino triangle

so of course
we're funny — it's what

we have
instead of checks and balances, what

allows us
to coin in the shit

with a smile
in a dome

of bearish lavender
while pivoting

our ju-jitsu
ever inward.

XX. THE FOURTH WAR

Oh it's all great fun
in the corn maze
until someone gets lost —

earth art,
crop circles without
the laughs, digging

around in Drumheller
for Beefheart's
'dinosaur cold' —

inside the Holy Mountain
midsummer light
etches your profile

onto plywood as you sleep.
The assumption is that
the big important shapes, say

where shotgun
overlaps with two-stroke
to define rural metrosexuality —

Richard Boone in
Have Gun Will Travel
on a pimped out

Triumph on the Parkway,
raw from the abrasions
of his English Leather soap label,

an angled mustache
that still reads 'ex-officer'
from Victoria north to Campbell River,

whose neoprene longjohns
enable him to tough it out
until November,

or where rising fuel costs
temporarily trump
the fear of creosote & coalsmoke

to re-enable the choking fogs
that had disappeared
with the industrial base —

that all of this is safely tracked
from space, indeed
to be lost is ultimately

economic, those people
under the rubble assumed
their cell phones

would save them, an island
held in place
with mirrors, they

can hear you, they
can see you, they
just can't help you.

XXI. A LETTER FROM HAMMERTOWN
TO THE BOTTOM OF THE EAST RIVER

Well fuck you
Albert Ayler,
it is *so* about me —

if I could
leap the pommelhorse
of self I wouldn't

have failed gym,
let alone the real horses
I pemmicaned on field trips,

the chicken pavilions,
veal pens, the eels
I stashed without appetite, Creeley

reminds us
that all heat is derived
from some animal,

that deliberate misreading
ends in disappointment,
like Burgess Meredith

as Borges —
libraries are for losers,
no more than a bus passenger

controls the route
can we be said
to skate between the periods &

you & Shepp
& all the armies of death metaldom
could no more wake Enitharmon

than a brass clock
in an aluminum pail
struck by lightning.

XXII. A SPORTSMAN'S NOTEBOOK

Walking down Minetown
I surprised the covey of quail
you kindly braked for last spring —

grown some since! it starts
as a scare almost — boom — low low note
somewhere inside the startled flapping

a blossom in the thorax
a mirror-ball flash of upturned leaves,
no time for even a decent recount,

less than ten, more than four
but quail for sure, that short take-off leap
and then low bottle neck cormorant

underwater plunge about a foot up
from the tangled thirty degree slope then gone
but however fast it's the sonic boom

that arrives just after you do,
and anyone can learn to do that —
like that Aussie woman on the newschannel

you can dehumdify
the room until it matches
your preferred level of discourse —

the earnest western tweet
swept beneath lacquered feedback
with a smooth adjustment of the wrist,

the windows thrown open
onto a clean clear drink of water
forever and ever and ever.

XXIII. CAPTAIN HOOK

. . . by hook
 or by crook . . .

John Cale's
big career move circa mid-80's:

a majestic parade-float of
Procol Harum-ized

punk, but recorded live
real brittle-like —

a metallic board mix
chunky metal cassette mix

irritating
irritating

the 'loudness' button
remember that

it was for this
not the cushion

of even that *heimlich* distortion
re: Thomas's Pistols, Spector's Ramones

or even Motorhead —
if your ear accepts it

as other than assault
at any volume

irritation is just
ideological,

don't tell me
you can fit

the Stray Gators
into your helmet

and keep on riding! —
so in the midst of this

12 minutes of mock-epic opening
side 3 of the IMAX Thunderdome w/

Bowery ambience
subbing for the Edmonton Symphony

and Cale has come in character
Dick Burton at the beginning of iguana

with a miner's helmet
and a fistful of Arthur Janov

overmatched it proved
against the punks in their red brigade pyjamas

for who remembers Bobby Sands
& Frederick Forsyth paperbacks

& Walken
in the snow:

the mercenary chic
is what stuck.

SIX PHOTOGRAPHS BY
ADAM HARRISON

Written as catalogue text for 'Examples of Photography,'
CSA Space Gallery, May 2006.

I. COVERED WINDOW

The skin of it puckers
and pools in lenses
bleached at the knots

a kind of drapery I guess
though oxidised
it might be the sun

but not real broke
not theatrical sugar broke
like that bottle trick

from TV, trinkle tinkle
of loops recorded
by guys long dead —

late for work
heads wrapped
in vinegar paper,

copping some attitude
with the bitches
in the mailroom, givin' it

the old watercooler
one-two — 'I done
it for the *in-surance*' —

Well wave goodbye
to the glove
factory, girls;

fifty arches
of brick-cladded
rustbelt gothic

but only
the dollar store
in focus, trade goods lit

so sharp thru the fog
you could read
the shampoo instructions

from a passing bus
and still huff
on a candle bag,

deserted dairylands hiss
warm Coke rings of
green styrofoam here

like everywhere else,
arboreal shrinkage hiss
farmhouses curled

on wet glass,
north of pine nuts the
little trees eventually

damage the little
touches we like;
the windows replaced

with particle board as
if mushroom carpets could
think mushroom thoughts.

Trade goods
rinse and repeat
and repeat.

You see, I want
to be part of it
but I want to

make fun of it too —
concealing profits or
making a bed of them,

stuffing a turkey with it
or smashing it with a brick —
whose answerable needs met?

II. LEAVES

Non-seasonal growth,
including the ludic
branches that clutch
the canopy's light breeze —
    no beach so fierce!
Or on top
of the cobblestones
the *picture*
of a beach, after
naming the streets
for the days of the week
we did trees, birds
Manitoba college towns
and then ran out so
started right in
on the spawn of
the local bauxite
aristocracy, so it's
possible to awake
with a familiar name
pressed into your cheek —
    something to fool
the *eloi* archaeologists!
presuming they can cut
through the giant hedge
of modified alder
that threatens Edwardian
apocalypse to these
pretty but blandly
peopled avenues.

III. WASHING MACHINE

The weather
phones it in

spring's a little
indicating this year —

a barrel of apples
without a retake, but

anywhere upstage
past act three is

a forest of elbows,
Sen-Sen breath

with little bites
attached: —

engorged
like the lines of force

in a woodcut windmill
watch the washing machine face

spin out of character:
the miracle of half-price Tuesday

carved out of
the larger miracle of laundry

through condensated
gaps rubbed

brown pigeons
with white chevrons

drop radar tinsel
on armloads of cashmere,

*Reader's Digest*s
limp as kid leather

skitter wounded-bird
style dropped with intent

on enameled trays for
generic pop, ashtrays

and exits
spotwelded, but

oh for the billows
and billows of hot steam

to hide the
anthropomorphic array,

the green stalkers
in the park,

the variously angry
smug, gleeful,

anxious, stoic
and startled faces

of the babies, the leaves
and the cars.

IV. CONDENSATION ON MIRROR

Kavanagh's *bright*
shillings of March
well spent for *aince*:

conker string,
a brand-new set of clackers,
a towel that becomes

a sleeping cat then disappears,
a camera that puts the silver
back into the lake, all those

pets and old uncles released
from whispering branches
and skins of chrome

to fistfuls of earth
and muscular sepia —
never to be recorded otherwise,

like the mound people,
sieved once through Toynbee's catbox
but never written down,

not even in steam
not even to spend a penny,
dredged up from a Murphy bed

into the coalsmoke
and cigarette smoke
and cabbage steam.

V. RAGS

Wilderness for welfare,
Athenians all in a little rank
we slipped out the back way

just glad to be of use, really
wiping up the unthinkable
with the untouchable —

a parachute of J-cloths,
linen liberated
for midsummer sneezes —

otherwise they'd be diving
under their desks! reaching
around for the comical

golden shred, the
big booty polish.
Cooking up Woolite

with Worcestershire
in hammocks of lint
the last stage in the life

of an honoured object,
soaked with sap and
strained through particle board

as the world of print
sulphurously beckons;
each thing eventually the receipt

of itself, each hanky
bearing a needlepoint letter
more easily felt than seen.

VI. CHINESE LANTERNS

In a poplar mist
a polar opposite

trumps intelligent design
through sheer forfeiture

anecdotally
like that guy in Mann's

Faustus —
the shells must

be saying something!
all those curlicued glyphs

and painted
bells!

let alone these
Boundary Bay sandcoilers

we're erasing
underfoot *get*

the luminol
later, you're shedding

Linear B here
a whiff

of red clay
a transparency

assumed then lost,
our faces

scanned as Cobbett would
scan a prospect from his mule,

(hay rots in the field —
thanks all night euchre/

Methodism,
it hardly matters)

and then a blunt assesment
bluntly deliver.

For you to touch the remote control
you have to touch

yourself first, but its
hardly a matter

of first causes,
tiny traces left are

not in themselves
an offense, and if

the endless and softening
imprint of appearance

avails thee not
what of it?

The ghosts
are knickers

in the trees,
sky pink

as an innocent
Christian ham ...

HOMAGE TO DAVID HOLZMAN

In Jim McBride's 1967 fake documentary DAVID HOLZMAN'S DIARY *there is a scene where Holzman (L.M. Kit Carson) mounts his 16mm camera in front of his television sometime before the evening news, firing off one frame every time the shot changed until sign-off. On film this lasts for a second or two but slowed down on VHS it became a clickable photo album of mid-60s TV. These timed readings are offered in that spirit.*

24.4.06   1215 – 1222 HRS

In black and white a man
looks at a family photo, wooden
church against a tearful

North Dakota sky, a slightly
dwarfish granite
Helmcken addressing

from a cozy gothic
portico an empty corner
of our dozing capital

while the insistent
Liona Boydalike strums
Vivaldi for Pursesnatchers.

Sobbing with emotion
through the *Zapp* setting
of a friendly vocoder

a man in long extensions
addresses a young woman
in denim shorts

who sits on a sportscar
hood — everything is
murky bluegrey monochrome

except their yellow
shirts and the red
of the car, the hems & glottal

hesitations of the
simultaneous translator
are likewise the sound of thought,

something a vocoder
might seek to blur
much as Mike Harris —

nostalgically glimpsed
lying his ass off
at the Ipperwash inquiry — might,

with the kind of quasi-medicated
brutality that can only be
acquired in a boyhood

marinated in cheap schoolyard
betrayal, seek
to blur adult emotion with

the sound of newspapers
flopping against a wet deck.
You're the kind of

girl that can see beyond
my poultry but still
fit into my world, not

the kind of a person that
would bring _____
to an anger-management

potluck in a community
already seething
with _____.

'I'm a nervous wreck this
salad spinner is making
me a nervous wreck.'

A prematurely middle-aged
boy actor, seated, is addressed
by a standing Barbara Stanwyck
whose hands brush the marbled lintel
of a fireplace lit to look like a slab
of obsidian but he seems terrified
beyond the demands of the scene
standing up and falling into
her arms as if obeying an offstage
slap he twists in her embrace
away from the camera
'Oh Keith!' and across her face
a discomfort registers that is as
cold and clean as Brooklyn tapwater,
a continental squaredance,
an old school shudder of purest modernity
as horizontal as the ultra-brimmed hat
of the athletically prim
police spokeswoman gold
OPP shield on it as big as the
sunny side of a duck egg on
a bed of distressed spinach,
the voice of the reconstruction
sounded like a morning's
work for one actor
doing 'voices' without enthusiasm,
for not enough money in
a Burnaby closet wrapped in felt
while the girl from Wayne's World
who has (Eddie Cantor-like) been
transported to Roman times
addresses the senate —
and you're the senate.

From its nest
on a plate of ruffles

the head of Greer Garson
acidly advises Joan Crawford

'we're all *that kind*
of woman, getting tired

of things we're used to —'
while a dog lamp with a bobbed fringe

throws a grey-scale corona
onto the omnipresent

MGM roaring glowing fire &
then it gets good because

the dolly toward Garson
goes into the news crawl's

comprehension-free swoop
and comes out moving

toward an empty wingchair and
another fireplace before

coming to rest on a copy
of Michener's coffee-table *USA*

resting on a coffee-table.
Let me put a dime

on the tone arm of
that for you, dad — less

time in the men's room
and more time fishing, less

time squeezing the clock and
more time punching the cilantro —

the 'matrix drip'
means that the information

wants to step forward
in a way that suggests the

carefree tinkle of glass beads,
just as the ascending blue

bar pulse Data was 'looking'
at yesterday likewise suggests both

'time running out'
'breaking news',

a steady trickle of dye
into the watertable,

a lawsuit
reaching back from

Ektachrome gullies
to swamp the future —

colour colonizes
this riot footage

with nosegays of rifle fire
& wreaths of red wire.

27.04.06   1031 – 1055 HRS

From out of the orchestra
thirty-two years ahead of schedule
the Buddy Miles rat-a-tat-tat
as white letters shatter & drop
means full-on WB rococo is in effect —
Eddie G's the *good* guy,
Bogie in the middle of
his pre-*Falcon* 'cheap thug' slump
cracking wise halfassedly
thru the expository
mini-doc on how the mob adds
a cent to the cost of every asparagus
while peaches rot on
the sidings, meanwhile
Robinson stares at his immense
highball tumbler — thick glass, real
ice in it carved to look
like grapefruit segments —
pineapple juice with a
dash of grenadine lights like
a sidecar — rim of gold about an
inch wide & then just *drops*
the guy from a seating
position with a shinkick &
some sort of prewar ju-jitsu
twister to the midsection but
Joan Blondell could care less —
it's not something Little Rico
would have done!
Throwing a guy through
a glass door and joking
about it for the audience's
benefit a sign of lateness at Warner's
as sure as Cavafy panpipes
or the smirking gods of *CSI*
playing through our pain —
write the word BAM

64

in Sharpie & then wipe
it with a damp cloth fingering
the opulent tassle the frappé
tassle the Limoges tassle,
forced to spend every holiday
testing games for our dad
the game inventor presented here
in paradiso flashback
as a vaguely Sendakian bear
in a tweed suit
but they should have used more sun
or water-skis or something
because those varnished
little gamepieces rattling
and the silver balls rolling
over the kabbalistic carvings
bum me in a very
non-Ouija way.

Acid green nascar verges
lit from above in patches
the colour of lemon squash
consumed on the lip of a council estate
in the waning autumn of '68 —
coalsmoked terraces typewriter gray
granite in serried planner's ranks
inside played Jim Reeves, brown milky tay
or Hank the one with the guitar leaning
on a stool, Mario Lanza 'The Student Prince'
& Jimmy Shand or Andy Stewart
but never both, strict-time 45s
with instructions, bedrooms from which
Eddie Cochran had never been exiled —
piece & jam & the penetrative
warmth of the heater
so much more hell-like than crackling cedar
and those little devilled ham devils
dancing in the fake flames don't hurt
for the duration of a sixpence
and two sides of a single.

02.05.06   1211 – 1223 HRS

Ugly edit detergent waves through your trunk
Loop current through your arm and out your back
Loop current from the bottom of a well
Teddy's voice from the bottom of a well
Theo's beats from under the floorboards
'the love I lost'
but something about seeing
a picnic table all exposed on
its back like that made me look away,
and the screen filled with blue sky
just as the golf channel lost the ball,
then we watched it clear the Playmobil
treetops before coming to a soft rest
by a little lake with applause like ducks.

Mickey Rooney and Oz who's also
the last of the old school telegraphists
hand-eating coconut cream
& apple in the back office at night,
Mickey, 15, high-necked Cruikshank collar
his version of turn-of-the-century normal
means each gesture is unpacked
in a series of boxes wrapped in tissue:
how nice to see the great ones 'underplay' —
and leave off of Tim Holt by the way
his Georgie is what you're really like
and I'm really like let's face it —
pontificating with our mouths full of pie
as traffic and ignorance blot out the sky.

12.05.06   1420 – 1431 HRS

On the high-pixel version
of the new urbanism I guess we'd
be the puff of cloud clinging
to a chalet-speckled hillside
like Colonel Sanders goatee —
happy to be in the picture at all!
if not without the sheep's similar
critique of its meadow:
that it is not sufficiently flat,
that objects are not transparent,
for just beyond the folded rocks
— Doughty's 'heaps of witness' —
are the proving grounds
where *all* the styles are tested
& hard pretzel salt covers the trees
& the Easter Island faces of the dogs
glare up from helmets filled with milk.

THE AGE OF BRIGGS & STRATTON

I. THE AGE OF BRIGGS & STRATTON

A hammering
in the night
even after we'd finished

an arrythmic stroke
neither on the four
nor the one quite,

but pure tinkering,
that is
the ominous rattling

of inner distress
taken for molar
or fingerbone

rather than
design flaw, the mere
wear & tear

properly
natural
to a two-stroke so

innocent of
maintenance
but not sawdust not hardly!

that will accede
to pleadings, piques &
inappropriate invocations,

thus mow the lawn
ten seconds at a time
and curse the earth

with the hammer
as a wrench
or with a wrench

work boulders free
to lay the grid
of mulching pigs

over everything
erasing without squeal
the leafblower's legacy.

II. A POEM FOR TOFINO

At six o'clock
inside the Moose Hall
the first spaghetti
supper of the fall:
a word or thought
experiment gone awry
& the whole of Tuff City
went boneless dry; as
boilers and radishes
barged Alberni Canal
they found out the acquifer
was not their pal.

From Bremen they came,
zucchini kayak and a dream —
of walking sticks
with little badges
avocado wraps
with nothing added —
not to be told
to dig their own hole.
We voted you in
because we didn't need you —
we should have checked
your leaning lean-to —
& now the dew's bribed
off the lawn & from
infant eyes the tears
are drawn, the Empire's
here but the water's gone.

III. IL CONFORMISTA

A tentative big toe
dipped in the Cold Lake
of rapture but as short
of real immersion as
the old army game,
balls dropping unnoticed
into the back pant pocket
or something like that —
an argument bolstered
by mere proximity (clack) is
the reassertion
of a dialectic that
never was, that
between looking
for something &
just looking, say
Dominique Sanda
as sleek as a panther
which I then didn't get
favoring the pale brunette,
but the desire, however
'gripped', that links
junkie, riot, sugarcone,
the washed away &
the washed out is
what muscles us up
for Mussolini, the
'primal scene' in that sense
comes free with every
Kodak. That's why
its called 'software'.

IV. A LETTER FROM HAMMERTOWN

Only the densest
dentist insect overtones
dare drop into the valley

from the Sunday construction
so impatiently at ten begun above
though the rate of such things

varies more than you'd think:
some build as if session men
called out by the union

to short time the undergrowth
for the Xbox simulation
of the Birth of Skiffle, others

as if flown in on Blackhawks
to build an interrogation centre
five days ahead of the army —

outward facing polished tin walls to
conduct heat, spirit animals
laminated into every post for

low-grade hallucination
when the Red Bull & castor oil
kick in — others as if alders were

closing in with a green man's leering
face and that aggregate should
be poured down his throat right now.

Over in Townsite
evolved sparrows turn into lawn
ornaments at will &

the sleepy subsonic rumble
of Chase River thru the park is
unbroken either by the snap of skateboard

veronicas or the dream-
speech of dogbarks & east of that
the Kingdom of the Cranes and Spiders

occupies the Arena
where Fats Domino once stood
where the roll of the Second Line

& the two-four of the bass drum
echoed from the Foundry
across Newcastle Channel.

V. A LETTER FROM HAMMERTOWN
TO THE NINTH WARD

From the time he had shoes, he roamed the neighborhood
     (NIK COHN, *Tricksta:*
     Life and Death and New Orleans Rap)

Defective and partly invisible
as the pagination of a yellow thesis
loosening like dream-teeth
or niblets blackening on the grill —
a study of piracy as much as trade,
of simony as much as privacy,
of property as much as specie,
thus an alum farmer of Yorkshire
is exempted from impressment
by the same principle as sugar bled
from a tree implies crystallisation,
not seeing its fate in the sticky Smitty's window
the summer not quite even over.

For the monthly purpose
of re-upping the state of emergency and toward
the interpretation of shipwreck
we assemble in this playhouse
by the light of a gibbous moon —
& not a crumb or shred or macaroon
of what is said will leave this room . . .

Alka-Seltzer stars scattered on blue felt,
the good warm smell of a dog smoking a cigar
with Lady Luck and her 52 imaginary friends
found curled in the ditches with coffee ends,
no one wants the burnt dregs of the last card
with a hole burnt through or to eat their phone.

Everyone just wants to go home.

VI. L'ENFANT

Tough to find your centre
in Seraing in the winter
as Vinegar Joe drones CNN
the sublet won't even let your hand in —
but all God's children get a handbasket
a task, a handcart, a pot to piss in
& maybe a glimpse of a river masking
the smell *d'argent* with the reek of its absence —
we're all neo-realists, all sleek & handsome,
except for the babies pawned or ransomed
for cellphones & a wagon pushed through the wind,
like a masterless cub sans sword to spend
each day in the open and each night in a hole,
the leafless damp canyons a kind of parole.

VII. A LETTER FROM HAMMERTOWN

Dear _____,

If it's not my fault reggaeton
ain't catching on
with the surf & sandalwood set —
these 'sleeve notes'
as you call them
are still all that
keep me from following
Sunny Boy & Red River
over Pellagra Falls —
OK so never the chef
nor the entrepreneur,
but not the guy in a leather apron
with a bolt-gun either,
delivering up discrimination
at the end of a sticky fork
& if the molasses taste of anger
is likewise as brittle
when it cools off
as a guinea palmed to a retainer
at the moment of yearly eye contact
so too the pronouncements
of the Brazen Head
can pass in a dark room
for both nourishment
& judgement.

VIII.

So much of *L'Orphee*
plays in that grim middle-aged way
poor Spicer never lived to see
that it's like I know better;
ie Jean Marais is how we're
supposed to look on the *inside*
& those hoopleheads at the cafe
rioting over Johnny Ray
as Mrs. Mills tinkles at 78
& the Hugo Boss bike cops drop their mitts —
what Martian could have predicted an Elvis
emerging from their thin Huguenot gruel?
Why do the youngsters blame me?
Don't their radios get the CBC?

IX. THE SOCIALIST REVIEW STYLE GUIDE

Turns out syndicalisation
doesn't work any better for wooly bears
than verbal warnings or
white stripes worked for us;
the road these nutdrop noons
is just the warmest place around
as well as the hardest —
twenty feet of good Akenhead with a slight tilt
covered in shit and shiny shells
courtesy of Mr. Blue October here —
& even when they make it over the line
the berm is not permanent
and the fuckraking leafblowers
papercut the air into orange froth.

X. THE SEDENTARY MILITIA

. . . slowly the day turns
into one of those ruined sheds . . .
GERRY GILBERT

We built these postal districts
over the bones of the dead
because we didn't recognize them
until remote control
returned them to us
as eye-stuffing but static ritual —
Frank McHugh & Capucine,
Alec Baldwin & Bart the Bear,
rolling bones in the alley
behind was it the Archimedes Club,
The Old Flag Inn, The Ambassador,
The Outrigger, The Diner's Rendezvous?
Not even the sky uninterrupted
by their clacking sound
as the old machinery broke down,
& town stopped being 'town'
& the mountains got filled in
with mile after mile of drywall scrim
through which a poltergeist chopper
but not an untainted breeze could pass.

Cold was the heather
& colder was the weather,
colder still the reckoning —
Gulliver burgers & brown soup
over hashmarked bohemian rice
not far from where the very air
was unpacked & rendered
of its rhetoric, passed out
in the park for pigeon peas,
a yard of rotting pillow straw
ripped from home plate & turned
from the foot of Woodland
toward the bus stop.

X. THE CANADIAN TIRE FOOD COURT

One thing Lang taught Hitch
was that those UFA model cities —
etched in nitrate, moonshine
& black letter —
blow up even nicer
than the real thing;
chemical factory
monochromes layer
& unfold real slow & pretty-like
over receding heaths
til naptha flames flare
& spark to reveal
the Napoleon of Crime
in real time scratchin' &
working the curtains —
out of politeness really —
while turntables on strings
answer the phones &
forged fistfuls of Canadian Tire money
pour out of the call centre
into the pockets of a fifth column
nourished on circus-grade granola
& keno at the henhouse.

XI. ODIE ODE

Farewell dog not native to the valley
but like me too
an all-weather patriot
& devotee of its unbillable hours,
sans cats & purebred jogging helmets
with at least the possibility of chicken
in a broth from a ditch
made with something else living,
fur weatherproofed with
coal tar & sulphur until only
a rain of little punches
sunk into haunches
can wake the sleeping beast
from his dream of bacon.

XII. THE LAMB RAN AWAY WITH THE CROWN

Given her Pythagorean triad
says Babs in a houndstooth huntress
anima number its Judee
for John Dee the real hippie
in out of the rain with
the rest of the ensemble
in the eggskull cave
of a stormy *Gaslight* cash-in
set inside a giant cake
where the fake wrench-shaped scar
of the corrupt chemist
is paired with the real scar
on Bogie's upper lip —
in every scene
it's the only thing really 'lit' —
leaving his hands (he thinks)
free to wander at will
back and forth &
back and forth between
the poison milk on the table,
his thin silver belt,
a series of not quite lit
smokes & a half-inch
double thumbed
pantwaist insertion,
O he's guilty alright —
of mailing it in bookrate!
writhing in his wingchair
jabbing the air with prepschool tics
until shoulderpadded Alexis Smith
hipfirsts toweringly in
swinging her gold David Hume turban
chain & giant buckle around until
his cowering leaves nothing
but the baked light of North Hollywood
through the grey of the background
of the background of the grey hills

& appearing from behind
an oak screen a skinny arm
catching the last of it
with a pivoting mirror.

XIII. HANDS OVER THE CITY

A walk
on gilded splinters

in terrycloth
slippers

or felt like they
made me wear at Sans-Souci —

polishing the ancient slats
they should pay you!

quiet as a childhood spent
at Schiller's Cinecitta

except for the damned dubbing
the same six voices

in every other movie
we ever saw — *Barabbas*,

The Campbells Are Coming,
A Bullet For Django — RCAF base theatres

then a point of pre-multiplex
distribution somewhere

between 42nd St. &
the edges of the 'Old Colonial' circuit —

so that their unaccented studio
bark colonised my kidspace

bigtime even if I never
even heard Burt's authentic Palermo

grandee or the Calabrese
striver they must have got for Rod Steiger's

Neapolitan Robert Moses/
Donald Trump though

Rosi can't resist letting
him mime out a scene in an empty

office like something out of *The Big Knife*
volcanic method emotions

rubbing his face out
with a dampened hanky

with neck sweat for
lip-readers.

LIFE HISTORY

All poems in this section taken from appropriate volumes of the LIFE
HISTORIES *prepared by Arthur Cleveland Bent for the Smithsonian
between 1910 and 1954.*

I. WHITE NECKED RAVEN

'Quark, quark,'
they yelled, all in the
   while settling nearer, —
or so I fancied —
   till it seemed
as if they actually
meant violence.

   ★

As they often use
   old haywire
and cast-off barbed wire
   in their nests,
these cause short circuits;
this has cost
   one telephone company
$2,500 to $5,500
   annually to patrol the line
and keep it clear.

   ★

They pounded the air
   in vain effort
to outfly their tormentors,
   dove to the ground
but were forced
to take wing again,
   circled and beat
and tacked to no purpose,
and finally began mounting
steadily in big circles, taking
their punishment
   as they went, the
smaller birds keeping above
and beating down on them

in succession until
    all were specks
in the sky,
    and finally lost to view.

II. EASTERN CROW

The cooing
   was also given in the air

and on one occasion,
I saw a bird drop

slowly down
   with wings tilted up

at an angle of forty-five degrees,
singing as he fell.

   ★

Finally after
   many trials
she managed to arrange
a loose array of sticks
in the base
   of the fork.

   ★

I turned back at once
   as I had no desire
to disturb the birds'
slumbers but it
   was evident
that many,
even at this late hour,
had not settled down
for the night.

III. WESTERN CROW

It was the practise
   of the Crows,

after a hot afternoon's work,
   to spare themselves the trouble

of flying any considerable
   distance to water

by feeding
   on watermelons.

   ★

It is evident
that in such places

ducks could not carry
on nesting

operations
successfully.

   ★

The flock then rapidly
reacted to the changed
environment by abandoning
attempts at feeding from
the almonds and indeed,
by departing from
the entire region.

IV. NORTHWESTERN CROW

The old birds
   are easy to distinguish
for they sit quietly
in the trees
and gravely watch their young
at play.

   ★

If the wind is blowing,
they allow for the curve,

and usually do not make
   many misses

in their endeavor
to hit a certain boulder.

   ★

Their most characteristic
one is noted
when the old bird
is feeling especially foolish,
for they duck their heads
toward their feet,
and then give an upward tug,
at the same time
emitting a sound like
the pulling of a cork
from a bottle.

V. FISH CROW

Then away they glide,
from the trees
of the stream banks,

across wide plantations
of truck
gardeners.

★

He adds that they
   eat pears,
and are very fond of
   ripe figs;
they do considerable damage
to the latter
and have to be driven away
from the fig trees
   with a gun.

★

These the Crow
now before us

would frequently seize
with his claws,

as he flew
along the surface,

and retire
to the summit

of a dead tree
to enjoy his repast.

VI. HOODED CROW

From the tops
of the pine trees,

they ascended
to a considerable height,

when, hovering for an
instant, they would

snap up
an insect

and return
to near the former position,

remain for a moment,
and again make an essay.

★

When the observer
rushed up

from a distance
of about 400 yards

both eyes of the
unfortunate animal

had been pecked out
and it was dying,

apparently from injuries
inflicted on the brain

through the
eye sockets.

★

Critical observers
have not generally
considered that they

exercise any
intelligent selection
of hard as opposed

to softer surfaces
for this purpose;
nevertheless there is

evidence that in some
places they have learned
to utilize masonry

or walls
for their
operations.

VII. DUCK HAWK

Wings half closed now,
he shot down past the north end

of the cliff, described
three successive vertical loop-

the-loops across its face,
turning completely upside down

at the top of each loop,
and roared out over our heads

with the wind rushing through
his wings like ripping canvas.

★

Just above the water
    the hawk suddenly
accelerated, tapped

the cormorant lightly
    on the back, then
circled easily away,

while the frightened
    quarry took refuge
unharmed in the water.

★

At last as one turned
to evade the rush,
the hawk swung over
on its back,
and reaching
up one foot
as it shot by,
caught the swift
in its powerful grasp.

VIII. EASTERN PIGEON HAWK

How closely
they huddled together,
as if seeking mutual
protection,
but he went
right through the flock
and came out
on the other side
with one in each fist.

★

Holding it forward
and downward

in one foot,
it occasionally bent

down its head and
tore off a bit

without slackening
its speed.

★

All the while
the Titlark
was nearing,
if by devious
courses,
a dense
thicket
of alders
into which
it plunged at length,
to be seen no more.

IX. BLACK PIGEON HAWK

He swung on one,
and when the gun cracked

the bird started falling
in a diving, fluttering

flight, appearing
to have a broken wing.

★

The hawk
struck the snipe
squarely in
mid-air,
then quickly
carried it away.

★

Thus the successive
lungings and chasings
were not either one-

sided or haphazard,
but so conducted
that each bird alternately

took the part of pursuer
and pursued, and when
enacting the latter role

gave way at once,
or after the merest pretence
of resistance, to flee

as if for its life, dodging
and twisting; yet it was
prompt enough to rejoin

the other bird at the end
of such a bout, when the
two would rest awhile

on the same stub, perching
only a few feet apart
and facing one another,

perhaps not without
some mutual
distrust.

X. EASTERN SPARROW HAWK

The point of the beak
is sunk into
the base of the skull,
and the skull
is torn off
with a swift
forward motion.

★

Then, sometimes
   with a precise adjustment

to the force of the wind,
   it stops the beating of it wings

and hangs as if suspended
   in complete repose and equilibrium,

seeming to move not a hair's breadth
   from its position.

★

Perched on dead stumps
by the side
of the cottonfields,
   flying off
from the wires
along the track,
   hovering above
the bare brown stubble,
   we see them
again and again,
nearly always alone.

XI. DESERT SPARROW HAWK

The grasshopper is held
much the same
as a child would hold
an ice-cream cone.

★

Flies are
repeatedly rejected,

even if
the bird is hungry.

★

In flight, the sparrow
hawk was silhouetted against
the evening sky

and its extended talons
could plainly be seen
clutching the body

of the little bat,
whose wings appeared
to be folded.

XII. CHICKADEE

Enlivener
    of our winter woods.

   ★

The chika is,
as a rule, two tones
higher than the dees,
and the pitch is
B on the chika and
G on the dees, in the
next to highest octave
on the piano.

   ★

They made aiming
almost impossible,
for every time I raised
the rifle, one or two
birds would perch
on the barrel
completely hiding
the sights.

   ★

'Any old
side up
without
care'

   ★

blind man's bluff
and hide and seek,
and tag

and tag

when
staged in three dimensions

a labyrinth of
interlacing branches for

hazard

and swinging
underneath, caught
each end of the caterpillar

with a foot
so held it
fast

within a few feet
of its apple-branch door

calling *Hear, hear me*
with only a breathing space
between repetitions

caught by a cat
at Belvidire, N.J.,
on December 24, 1932

I wrapped the offending
rag around the branch . . .

    ★

The tail moves,
   the expanding
wings shoot
   out sideways
and strike the
surrounding wood
inside the cavity
   and as the head comes
stiffly down
the bird

emits a strong
hiss or puff
strikingly like that
    of the copperhead.

XIII. CHICKADEE AND TITMOUSE

At the moment
   of the lunge,
the black-and-white
   striping
of the head
   brought her into
abrupt and conspicuous
   view of the observer
peering into
   the cavity —
reinforcing
   the surprise effect
      of the sounds produced.

   ★

on June 9, 1935
go down
a little squirrel hole
underneath
   a dead pine stub
in a little clearing

of these the kinglets are

when the emotion of spring
   is no longer controllable
when the birds are obscured
   by the falling snow

   ★

he is omnipresent,
even in the heart of the city

{Brownsville}

on the inside
of the left mandible
of the huge
Sulphur-bottom
Whale skeleton
   under the shed

so he worked
   around my ear
and feel him snip snip
as he severed them

like the whistle
of a man calling his dog

he is omnipresent,
even in the heart of the city

{Brownsville}

   ★

the heavy, dark forests

{Kirkland}

on bending branches,
vent squeaks
and low chirps,
varied with buzzing
   'dizzes'

pairs thus continue
   up the forest-clothed flanks

of slopes and cliffs

only the blue jay
refuses to make way

brown above
and plain gray

{Kirkland}

the heavy, dark forests

THE GREAT NORTH

I. THE UPPER PENINSULA

Such strawberries as these
need to be seen

to be appreciated and must be
visited to be seen,

for they are too large and
too delicate

to bear much travel
themselves.

★

A cold ragged-trousered arrival
we had of it, into such weather

as would strip us clean
we thought, the bell bottom

bottoms likewise unhemmed
the better for to drag sticks

along like the furrowing bellies
of a fat clumping cat,

less walking than a kind
of controlled trip through

skinned coffeemate puddles
to unwaiting basements

and uncontrolled thaw.
To open the window

was to invite death, or if not
a long snooze in the Legions

of North Battleford, Cold Lake,
Pickle Lake, Humboldt —

anyway as far up as Basic Stick
had taught the locals to hip shuffle

& in appreciation buy beers
for the band including retinue.

Later Jerry Lee, Haggard, *Kind of a
Drag* & *Kind of Blue*.

    ★

It is the name
of a river, a canoe trip

down which
has all the charms

of wood life
without its discomfort.

    ★

Last dependant leaf
swinging like a rusty gate

or a kid's emphatic
no way headshake

getting carried away
& falling into an earthquake.

II. ON SNOW SHOES TO BARREN GROUNDS

The storm
was now squarely
in our teeth,
and the dogs
would not face it.

★

Face the skin & snap of it,
like business cards or snowpeas hurled
at the eyeteeth but hitting the lenses,
suddenly your wig is tighter
than your pants, forepaws
caked with frosting
palming meatballs past numbness —
your gold watch is
we don't eat you,
but the bear
or its surrogates needn't twig that!
But even not knowing the handshake
you could walk these Druid Hills unmolested
sneakers painted with lime,
breath neutral to minty,
predator smile projecting
a half-step ahead as
the plane tree tops of Coffey Park
poke and wave through the ice . . .

★

These people
had never before
seen a camera, and
many of my plates
show them scurrying away
or turning their backs.

★

Waves of wax
ebbed over the fly
until at last
he supplanted the wick
and burned on the counter
for over an hour.

III. HUNTING THE GRIZZLY BEAR

The poor idiotic boy
could not even then
realize the danger
through which he had passed,
and could only appease his anger
by continuing to maul
the bear over the head
with the camp kettle
for several minutes
after she was dead.

★

Thus from the rococo woods
stumble into the mannerist clearing

or is that muskeg
into which our hooves sunk

sucked runners off escaping subjects
replacing chickens with used books

so slowly no one noticed
until their cakeless birthdays rolled around —

on the icon they've got baby Jesus
standing upright in a dear little

Jjunior Pantocrator outfit —
orb & mace, little brocade robe

heavier than him, looking up at his mum
who looks through me.

★

Bears are usually,
though not always,
killed at considerable distances

from towns, or even ranches,
where it is not easy
to find a pair of scales.

★

Still hunters of the lyric
must shower with carbolic
to erase the stench of patronage,
build their hides with beaten pewter
to deflect the low winter sun's
dust-revealing torch
as it plays on yellowing pads
& capless brown markers,
they must fold their arms into little wings
and pretend to sing.

IV. STUBBLE AND SLOUGH IN DAKOTA

The happiness of a hunting party
is like that of a wedding,

so important is it
that true love shall rule.

★

A crow flies through
the tinkle of the last window on earth
carrying in its beak
the clementine eye of God,
around his neck a Diana set to bulb
the nitrate views of Minot
the deep sturgeons of Superior
Red Hills of death & indebtedness,
iron pocked surface with fake bulletholes,
elevators tight with mustard, canola, durum,
evolving past kingship with a penitential swoop.

★

The sun has set,
and no longer bathes
the landscape
in its golden light,
and yet I sit
in the water and mud
and indulge this pleasurable
taste for gore, wondering
why it is so ecstatic,
or if my companions
will not give over
shooting presently.

★

Cut it out of your thoughts
as though snipping
the furball dreads

from a feral angora,
roll it out the snowy driveway
into the path of a boxy 4x4
with homemade chains
snapping & scattering in the ice,
press it to a wafer
in a tower of turtles.

PAGES FROM THE CHILDREN'S ENCYCLOPEDIA

for Michael Szarpowski & Bruce Conkle

I. CASCADIA BORDER PATROL

I'd like to stop kicking,
but every time I do
something spectacular happens

that people will pay to see —
it's not like its even down to me,
& running my fingers counting

bribes along envelope tops
hurts me as much
as these January pellets

raining from my winkle-pickers
must hurt you, but
Centralia's where the Inland Empire

meets the real Empire &
you've entered our domain
as an ark of infinite sustain —

orchards hazy with
ciderblink down to
Dorn's sound, lowering chopper

heat differential maps
of backpackers loaded
versus ornithologists

lightened by self-hypnosis,
though in real life
if surveillance gets

that close it's probably what's
in your thermos
they're after.

II. CRANBERRY FIREHALL

Stinks to be in the engine
of always conspirin' & pokin'
where it *ain't* exactly required —

rattlin' around like a tooth
in a paint can achin' for inspection,
but like the firehall's multi-function

a ramp into space
is no longer an option,
no fire escape in the sky —

they're mixin' the gravity with somethin'
or somethin' — but it's still a good thing
the lid's this big, you turn it right down

step out onto the 'scape
for a couple of cupped Cameos & voila!
when you return everything

is exactly the same
except it's ready now,
wreathed in glistening steam!

III. ENTIAMORPHIC CHAMBERMAID

A stack of *Argosy*
in an orgone box,
but no bacon
in the midden —
individually a dry maple leaf
in good nick seems
worth about a quarter
but I'll get rid of it
for a dime and put the change
in a Crown Royal bag,
and in the spring
a parcel of mulch
will arrive by courier;
less an operating system
than Rick Wakeman
vs. Dr. Who at Joddrel Bank,
more something slipped into,
all warm & well-rehearsed,
all long exhalations uncoiling
like Gilray speech balloons,
though the unfamilar tread
tenderizes ankles on the icy slopes.

IV. THE WIRE

Then the tree if not time
at least Art Blakey —
hard bop with a touch
of the parade ground,
in a good way —
the orderly handling by
many bird species
crowded up amongst
the short-term food
emergency — giving way
on the good branches,
keeping beefs short etc. —
then everybody gets their
designated seconds of
bark digging umolested
maybe some eavestrough
spider web, but stepping up
clean and bright
in bandstand order with
a solo worked up ahead of time
so that routine becomes display
and spring can start to operate.

V. THE DAWN IN BRITAIN

Fax addresses
other fax in fax

*'titivates with plumes
of voodoo jargon'*

AKA *'speaks in tongues'*
the mellow ameliorants

of mormon d'esprit,
lodge-blue, cop white,

pink snow, halfhard hotdog
bun cigar-angled

the raven's new year
accessory of choice

they get them 'from the farm'
whatever that means —

we've seen the rendering truck
stagger under towers years past

bundled like newspapers
now that presumptive hogs

are rarely present —
the old neighborhood herd

thinned to unemployability —
dogs, cats & fish —

hence other people playing cards,
golf, the film on baby foxes

in both official languages
with the sound turned off,

it's all to calm you down,
with at Xmas halfraw turkey

thawing by the 'fire'
to sink your teeth into

while a song we all know
encourages wordless grunting

suffused with emotion &
the heavy wine of childhood.

VI. PUNISHMENT PARKWAY

I suppose the scenic route
is out of the question —
too much time

by lay-bys earlier
running our elbows
along the bunched steel map

of braille mountains
worn through at the ocean
& where the ②️ passed through

amenable space you stand
at the edge of
the whole thing a ribbon

of iron control extending
even to the lichen's fluffy edge
so that to stray

is to fall into
the literal orchestra pit
after a Big Drop —

the vast
arbutus forest preserved
on either side of it

certainly terra incognita
before they put the highway through —
but Northfield was a labyrinth

out of Floyd Crosby's Poe
anyway so excuse me
if I never found it but

the immaculate moss meadows
argue that no one much
else did either —

there's a lot
of places dirt bikers
it turns out won't go —

but this civil terrarium though tidy
was roamed by giant tapirs once,
by badgers big as bears,

undisturbed by pneumatics
or the shrieking steam of the factory whistle —
must now endure

the lapidary condescension
of highway patronage, the cement lobby's
largesse, the planner's *passion*,

the grim and anxious trucks
from which the tongues of mammals
brush the pre-Cambrian air.

VII. CRAZY RHYTHM

To speed up
or slow down at will
like that
like Anita no matter
the lyric's 'arcs'
or who you're playing with
or in what vehicle careering
depends on the services
over decades
of a drummer —
Roy Haynes & Sassy
would be another
example — capable of lowering
six whirring brushes
onto a linseed-darkened
dream sideboard
while defending a perogy
supper from a platoon
of gibbons — imagine
having such a pedal to press!
messing with the band
would just be the start —
to feel the tin-pan-alley world
snapping like a green twig
but how tough after
negotiating now that speech
is king again the cabless dawn.

VIII. IKEA DESERTA

Leave sleep to those
in charge of sleep,
the bus he knows the way;
the pussycat anarchists won't
blow up the viaduct tonight —
you can rely on me.

★

On mattresses masters bestir cosily
by threadcounts unmolested
noisily, easily, easily, noisily —
but otherwise untested.

★

Planet it up for the business
of orbiting dirty snowball courses
what tirebiters flicked at cops,
nothing is as still as this sentence
which I began a million days ago
lifting myself onto the bamboo hula
while laces dragged the Barents Sea,
to wake folded in the folds of Forfar
in full dark stars coiling
mystic pools of social housing
& ghosts in full monologue
& all of it melting
not into green icing
but holes which are then patched over
with similar stuff
taken from elsewhere.

NEW STAR'S POETRY LIST